The Artful alphabet

Abba   Dash

For Pete

THE ARTFUL

P

L

A

First U.S. edition 2003.

Library of Congress Cataloging-in-Publication Data
Jirankova-Limbrick, Martina.
The artful alphabet / Martina Jirankova-Limbrick.
–1st U.S. ed.
p. cm.
Summary: Illustrations representing each
letter of the alphabet reveal a variety of
objects for the reader to identify.
ISBN 0-7636-2187-0
1. English language–Alphabet–Juvenile literature.
[1. Alphabet.] I. Title.
PE1155.J57 2003   2002072887
428.1–dc21

10 9 8 7 6 5 4 3 2 1

Printed in Italy

The text of this book was hand-lettered by the author.
The illustrations were done in ink.

Candlewick Press, 2067 Massachusetts Avenue,
Cambridge, Massachusetts 02140

visit us at www.candlewick.com

CANDLEWICK PRESS
CAMBRIDGE, MASSACHUSETTS

HABET

a в
б

Martina Jirankova-Limbrick

a

Apples

attention

acrobat

Arena

Aa

Aargh

Applause

assistant

action

audience

accurate

aim

arrows

Balloon

birds

Bushes

Basket

-i-n-g-   -b-o-u-n-c-i-n-g-

bridge

bees

B

b-o-u-n-c-

BUSY

BUSY

BUSY

BUSY

BUSY

Can   CAN'T   Cannot   CAN   Catch

CANNOT   CATCH   CAN   catch

Catch me
if you can . . . . .

Can't   can

          can

          CATCH   Can

               Can

.....catch.......me.....

castle

crossroads

cabbages

cake

cushion

Desert

Dominoes

Drum

D●t

D●t

Doll

Dice

Door

Dragon's Den

Dachshund

...dancing with a dragon...

Equilib

ENoRMoUS
ELEVATED
ELEPHANT

rium

every e
evening
exquisite
exercise
excuses
eyes & ears
excellent Ehd eee

e

ear

e e e ě e
e ě e

e

EXQUISITELY
EXHIBITED!
EVERY EVENING!

forest

FUN

fan

for

FRIENDS

Fish

Flute

flippers

fishing

flies

flying

Fountain

frog

floating

Fish

fountain

feathers

fingerprint

illustration

ice

intelligent

i

IDEAS

i

iiii

ICE CREAM

inside

ideal

iiiii

invisible

impossible

Incredible   Illusion

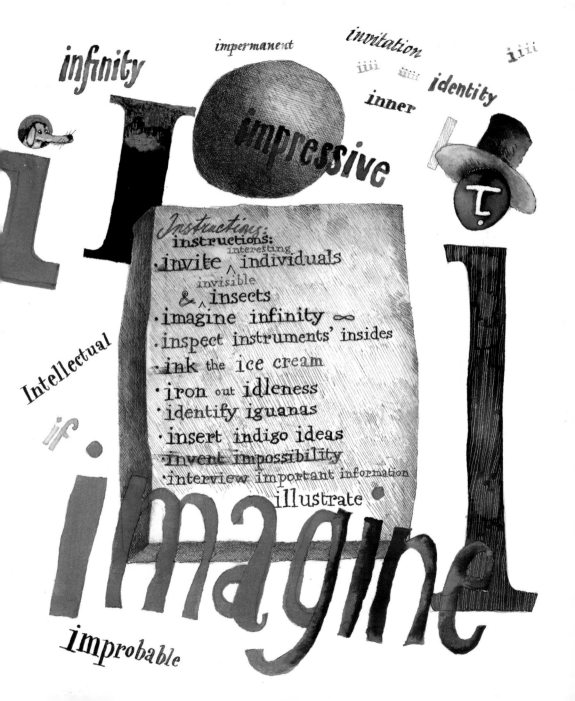

KISS

kaleidoscope

key

Kick

knot

knees

King

kangaroo

knitting

MOON

Monkey

Mirror

MONKEY IN MARBLE

MONUMENT

MAZE

ENTRANCE

M

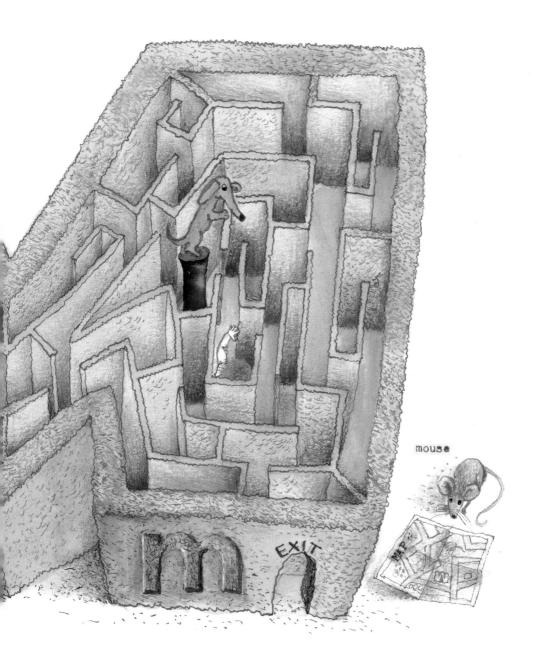

mouse

EXIT

Names:

Nick Norman Nicole

Natalie

Nancy

Neil

Nigel

n n n n n n n n n n
n n n n
n h h
n n n n
n n n n
n

Nest
nest Neil
Nest
NEST nest

night

news

nonsense
News

newspapers

newest

news

No News

nonsense Nn

11111 111
22222 2222222
33333333333333
4444 4444
5555 5555
6666 6666
777 777
8888 8888
9999999 9999999
0000000 0000000

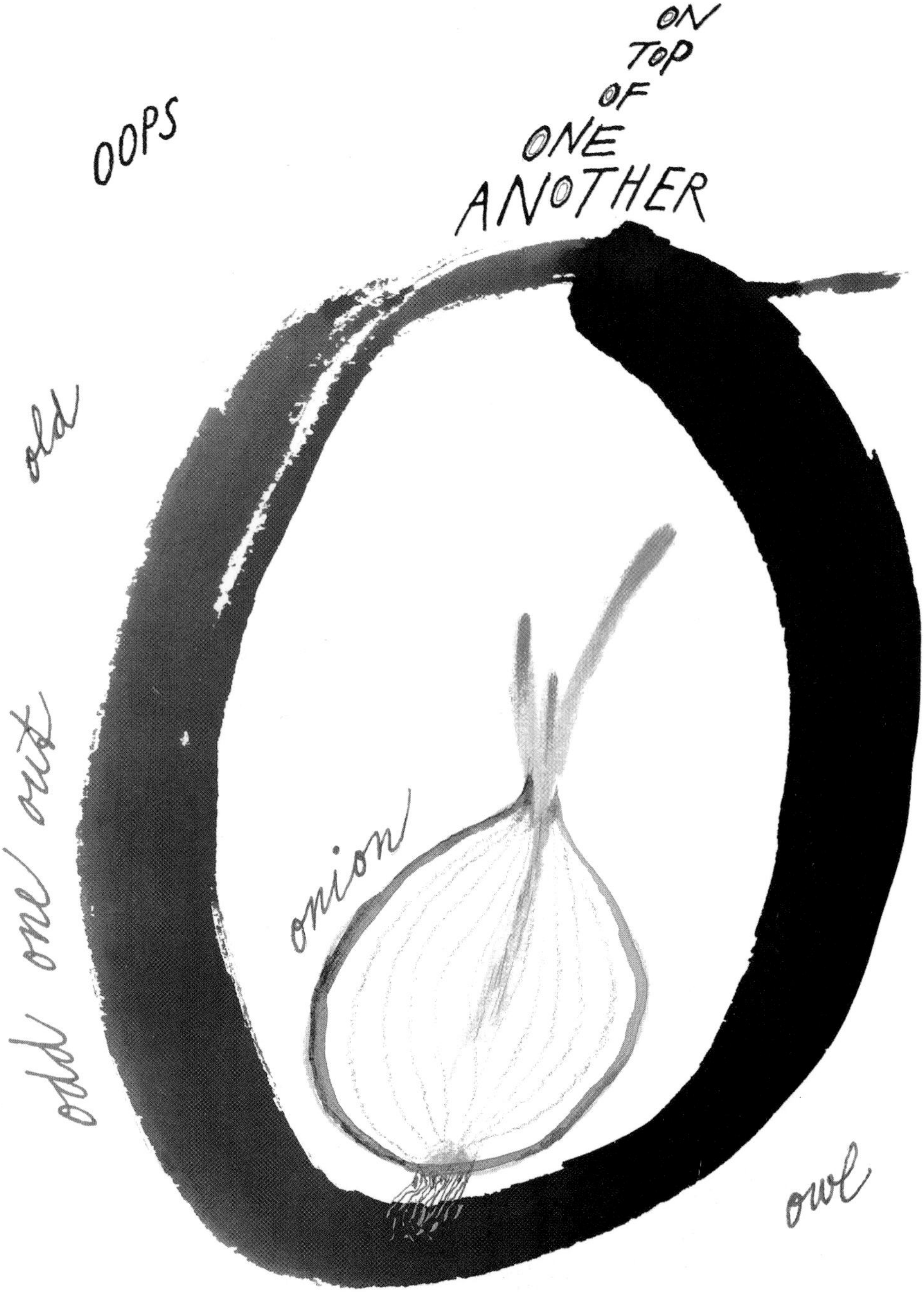

OOPS

ON
TOP
OF
ONE
ANOTHER

old

odd one out

onion

owl

oval

on

OOPS

OOPS

over

orange

patch

polka dots

pencil

PLEASE PAY HERE

Par...
Pauper...

PRINCESS

Punch presents personally production Preview parts...peopl
Perfect performance PUNCH Promising play PUPPETS
PARDON? Parable? Pigs pink pigs Pantaloons Patterns
Pantomime? Proverbs? Peacock's feathers Parchment Par

PUPILS parents Polite Posh & POOR
Playful PENGUIN peeping PREMIERE Pi
POSSIBILITIES patches Prop Promises
ardon? parrots? PIRATES! Present & past PAUPER PRINCESS

A bed-covering made of patchwork is sometimes called a?

?

What do four musicians make?

Q

A: Quartet

What is another word for a disagreement?

A: Quick

A TV game that tests what you know?

A place where marble is dug from the ground?

A: Queen

A: Questions

A: Quarrel

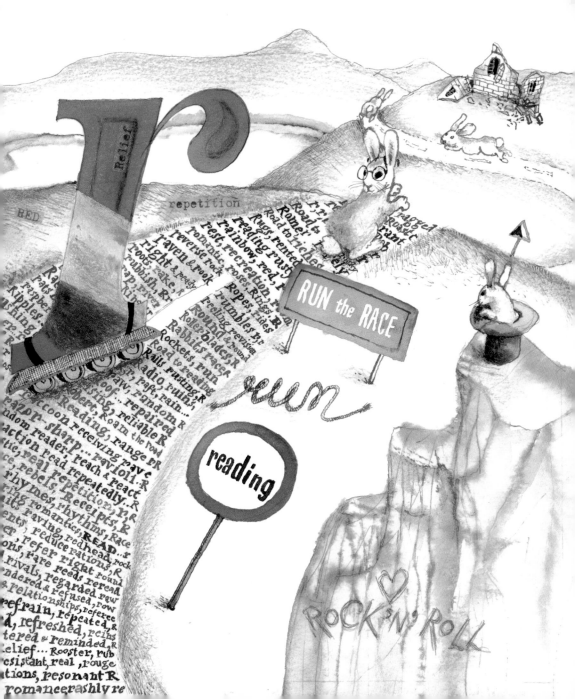

r
y
s
k
y

sleeping sun

S

shiver | stretch | swerve

scoot

splash

stop

skip

SPIRAL

slow down

skateboard

strange & silly

tightrope
tracks
tunnel
trumpets
try
text
triangles

topiary

TRAIN 23·10

TUNNEL

THINKING TIGER

underneath...

↑
up
↑
up
↑
up
↑
up
↑
Up

...uninvited unicorn...

u...u...u

truim [mrojin] umbrella uniforms unicycle ....up...up... upward Utopia unexpected

UTENSILS ique.USUAL...unicorn U-turn under underneath unclear...UNIVERSAL underground UNDERSTANDING upright utility

upside-down U

vvvvvvanish vvvvvv vanilla vv volcano v vast vvv veil vvvv vertigo

V valiant virtuoso verse vvvvvv variety vvvvv vertical v vertigo

vibrato vvv V vivace vvvvv

vvv vvvvv vvvvvvv vvvvv V voice vvvv

vvvv V Valentine V v very Vvvvvvv voice

vvvv V violet vv vvvvv

ing vVvvvv vegetable

V

W

WIND

WATER

WHITE

WILD

WONDER

WHISPER

X marks the spot

X

facing
ewa...ing
a exciting
a e
lynx
eXperience
eXit
eXercise
taXi
eXpert

bo...

o...ic

o...en

e...change

fo...trot

betwi...t

e...cellent

tu...edo

...ate

hoa...

fla...

cru...

pi...els

e...periment

ne...t

Me...ico

ma...imum

o...ygen

pi...ie

vexation

fixative

saxophone

X

fox

X-ray

he...

YAWN

YELL

YES

Yoga

Yoga for Y

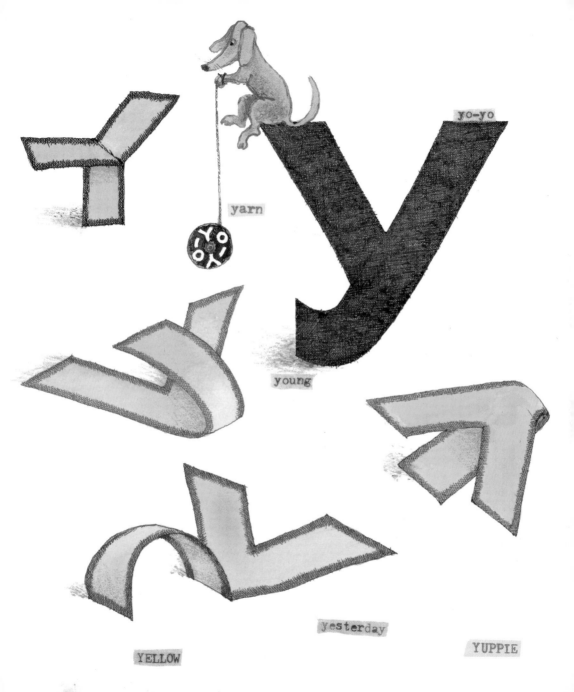

yo-yo

yarn

young

yesterday

YELLOW

YUPPIE

Did you *see these?*

dominoes
dome
dog
dice
desert

acrobat
apples
arrows
bandage
basket
bathtub
bed
bees
birds
blanket
bottle
boxing glove

cushion
clouds
clock
chessboard
chase
cat

castle

cards
cage
bubbles
brush
bridge
bricks

dress

 king

key kite

kangaroo

elephant

eye

jigsaw

jester

fan jay

fishing rod jaguar

fox  ice cream

 hippopotamus

geese hedgehog

hat

 hammock

goat

grass

ladder

lion

lollipop

mirror

marble

moon

nail

nest

night

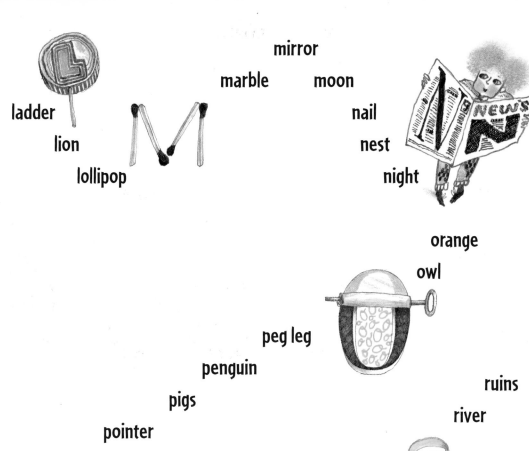

orange

owl

peg leg

penguin

pigs

pointer

puppet strings

ruins

river

rake

rainbow

"Q"

questions

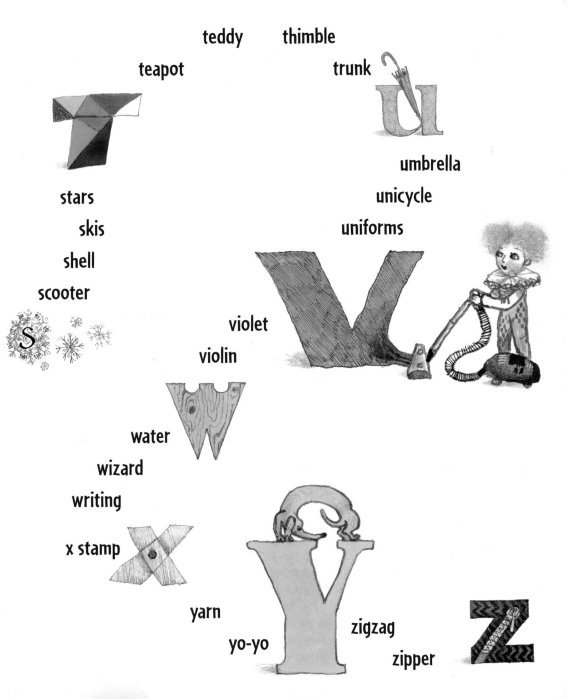

teddy thimble

teapot trunk

umbrella

unicycle

uniforms

stars

skis

shell

scooter

violet

violin

water

wizard

writing

x stamp

yarn

yo-yo zigzag

zipper

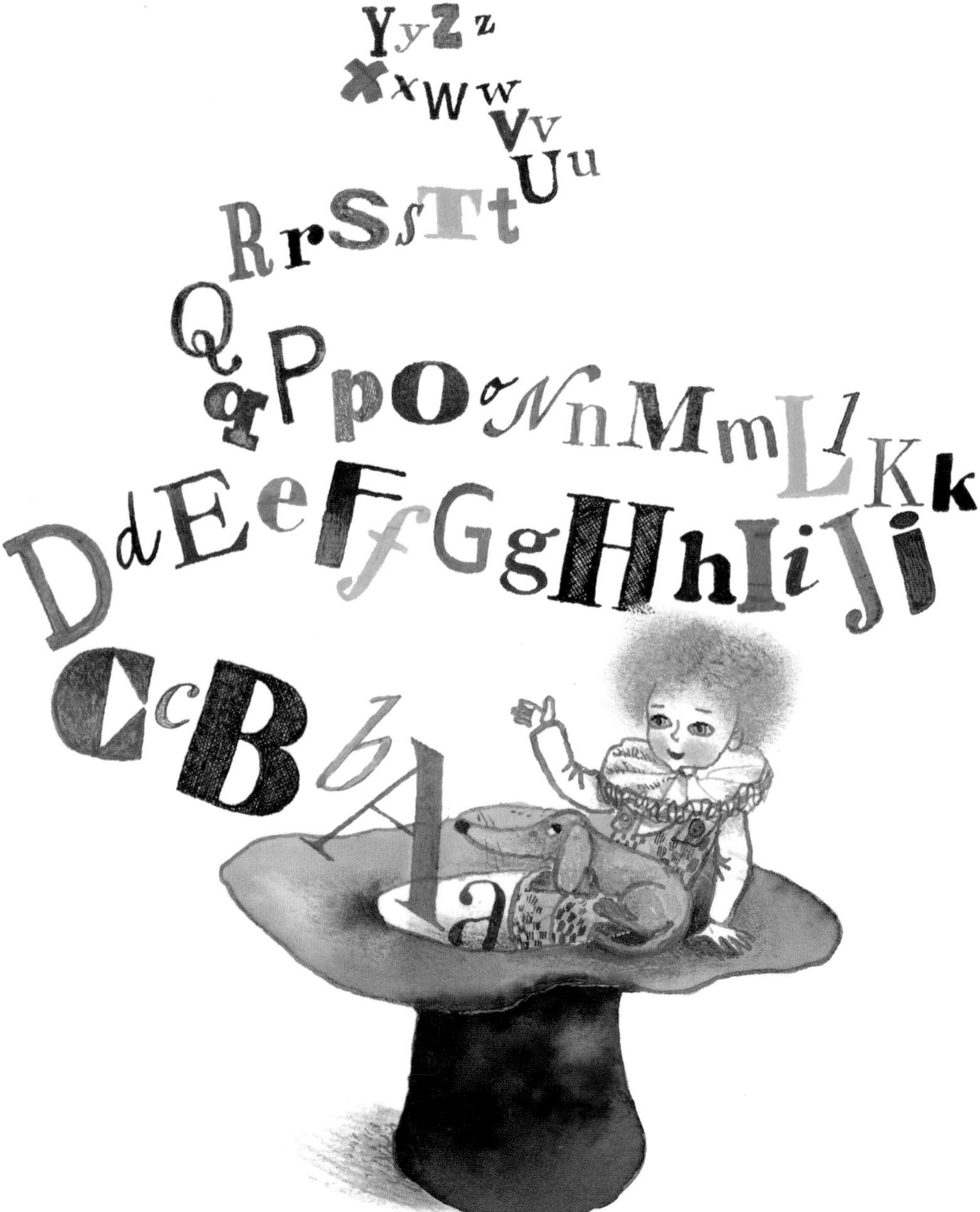